FAMILY

FAMILY

Biblical

TRUTHS

—

Around the Table

PUBLISHING GROUP

NASHVILLE, TENNESSEE

CONTENTS

CONTENTS

Somewhere along the line, the Bible attracted a reputation for being both irrelevant and impossible to understand. Out of touch as well as out of reach. Yet while conclusions like these continue to persist, so does human need for the Bible to be everything God affirms it to be: "living and effective" (Hebrews 4:12), its message "very near you, in your mouth and in your heart" (Deuteronomy 30:14).

If families are to live together in unity . . . if lives are to be whole and fruitful in heart and mind . . . if tragedy and loss and disappointment and confusion are to be survived . . . no, not merely survived but transformed into peace and power and a purposeful way forward . . . you need a Word that is here and now and able to be grasped. You need to "know the truth," because "the truth will set you free" (John 8:32).

That's why you picked up this book. You know the level of importance that Scripture needs in your home, and you are ready to take a step back, sit down, and soak in God's Word with your family.

Filled with Scriptures that speak personally to you, this little book is further proof that God intends His Word to share living space with your present reality. Always in touch. Always within reach. No matter where you are, or what you are going through, allow this book to help direct you to the Scriptures you need most.

ANGER

An unkind word, a missed dinner, a forgotten birthday. There are countless occasions in every family for anger to rear its ugly head. It's an emotion that we all feel and tend to feel often toward those we care about the most. The key is not to act out in anger, but remember the value of the family; and no matter what the cause of the anger, to always speak and act with love.

Refrain from anger and give up your rage; do not be agitated—it can only bring harm.

    Psalm 37:8

———

A patient person shows great understanding, but a quick-tempered one promotes foolishness.

    Proverbs 14:29

———

A gentle answer turns away anger, but a harsh word stirs up wrath.

    Proverbs 15:1

"But I tell you, everyone who is angry with his brother or sister will be subject to judgment. Whoever insults his brother or sister, will be subject to the court. Whoever says, 'You fool!' will be subject to hellfire."

Matthew 5:22

———

Be angry and do not sin. Don't let the sun go down on your anger, and don't give the devil an opportunity.

Ephesians 4:26–27

Lord, thank You for the family You have placed in my life. Right now I am holding onto anger in my heart. Wipe this anger out of me. Give me the peace and patience that I need to forgive. Remind me daily of the forgiveness that You have given me. I desire to love and serve my family well, but I know I cannot do this without Your guiding hand. Grant me the wisdom to know how to handle this situation in love. Help me to show love even when I do not feel it. Amen

Anxiety can come up in every part of our lives. Beneath our anxieties is a need to feel in control. Control in any relationship is impossible, especially when it comes to family. It is about give and take and releasing your control in exchange for relationship. Our peace is found in knowing that the Creator of the universe holds us safely in the palm of His hand and will protect us no matter the situation in which we land.

*"Therefore I tell you: Don't worry about your life,
what you will eat or what you will drink; or about
your body, what you will wear. Isn't life more than
food and the body more than clothing? Consider the
birds of the sky: They don't sow or reap or gather
into barns, yet your heavenly Father feeds them.
Aren't you worth more than they? Can any of you
add one moment to his life-span by worrying?"*

    Matthew 6:25–27

---

*Humble yourselves, therefore, under the mighty
hand of God, so that he may exalt you at the proper
time, casting all your cares on him, because he
cares about you.*

    1 Peter 5:6–7

"*Peace I leave with you. My peace I give to you. I do not give to you as the world gives. Don't let your heart be troubled or fearful.*"

John 14:27

———

Don't worry about anything, but in everything, through prayer and petition with thanksgiving, present your requests to God. And the peace of God, which surpasses all understanding, will guard your hearts and minds in Christ Jesus.

Philippians 4:6–7

———

For God has not given us a spirit of fear, but one of power, love, and sound judgment.

2 Timothy 1:7

Heavenly Father, sometimes my family overwhelms me with anxieties. I worry that I am not doing enough, or too much, or am not fully known or fully loved. Even though I know that I cannot hold the reins in a relationship, I still feel lost without some kind of control. Help me to leave my anxieties at Your feet. I entrust to You my relationships, knowing that Your peace will guard my heart and mind. Amen

Authority plays a part in every area of your life, and you simultaneously have roles on both sides of the equation, even within your family. When we exercise our authority over family members in love and humble ourselves to one another in submission, we are able to grow our relationships and strengthen one another. Seek wisdom in all your decisions from God, who is ultimately in control of every sphere of your life.

*Then he said to them, "Give, then, to Caesar the
things that are Caesar's, and to God the things
that are God's." When they heard this, they were
amazed. So they left him and went away.*

   Matthew 22:21–22

———

*Jesus came near and said to them, "All authority
has been given to me in heaven and on earth."*

   Matthew 28:18

———

*Let everyone submit to the governing authorities,
since there is no authority except from God, and the
authorities that exist are instituted by God.*

   Romans 13:1

For this reason God highly exalted him and gave him the name that is above every name, so that at the name of Jesus every knee will bow—in heaven and on earth and under the earth—and every tongue will confess that Jesus Christ is Lord, to the glory of God the Father.

Philippians 2:9–11

———

Submit to every human authority because of the Lord, whether to the emperor as the supreme authority or to governors as those sent out by him to punish those who do what is evil and to praise those who do what is good. For it is God's will that you silence the ignorance of foolish people by doing good.

1 Peter 2:13–15

Dear Jesus, I praise You for granting me wisdom and grace to be a mirror of godly authority to others; and I willingly submit to Your authority in all things. Father, give me guidance to know when You have called me to lead and when You have called me to submit. Create in me a humble heart, that even when I am in a place of authority I never forget that I still ultimately fall under Your headship. Amen

In the midst of chaos, it feels impossible to remember the blessings that God has placed in our lives. But even in the whirlwind, He is there. We can experience deep joy when we take notice of the abundant blessings in our lives and praise and thank the Lord for such bountiful grace, even in the midst of feeling overwhelmed. While running around, remember the provisions that God has given You.

"May the LORD bless you and protect you; may the LORD make his face shine on you and be gracious to you; may the LORD look with favor on you and give you peace."

Numbers 6:24–26

———

Indeed, we have all received grace upon grace from his fullness, for the law was given through Moses; grace and truth came through Jesus Christ.

John 1:16–17

And God is able to make every grace overflow to you, so that in every way, always having everything you need, you may excel in every good work.

2 Corinthians 9:8

———

Blessed is the God and Father of our Lord Jesus Christ, who has blessed us with every spiritual blessing in the heavens in Christ.

Ephesians 1:3

———

And my God will supply all your needs according to his riches in glory in Christ Jesus.

Philippians 4:19

Heavenly Father, I thank You and praise You for all the ways You have shown me mercy and grace, and I ask for the blessing of Your presence throughout this day. Thank You for the blessing of my family. Remind me daily of their presence, and do not allow me to take them for granted. Give me reminders today of Your goodness. Amen

Change is frightening. Whether you are mourning the loss of a loved one, preparing to leave a home you love, or even just finding yourself in a new stage of life, change can bring about high levels of stress and can put strain within a family. It may feel like if you can just move fast enough, and just do enough, you can control the change. But this is impossible on your own. No matter what the change is, the presence of God goes before you preparing the way. Have confidence that on the other side of this change, no matter what the new world looks like, God will be there.

*There is an occasion for everything, and a time for
every activity under heaven.*

    Ecclesiastes 3:1

———

*"Do not remember the past events, pay no attention
to things of old. Look, I am about to do something
new; even now it is coming. Do you not see it?
Indeed, I will make a way in the wilderness, rivers
in the desert."*

    Isaiah 43:18–19

"Because I, the LORD, have not changed, you descendants of Jacob have not been destroyed."
Malachi 3:6

———

Therefore, if anyone is in Christ, he is a new creation; the old has passed away, and see, the new has come!
2 Corinthians 5:17

———

Jesus Christ is the same yesterday, today, and forever.
Hebrews 13:8

Lord Jesus, I do not know what the future holds for me and my family, and it fills me with fear. I know that this stress is not the end of my story, and that You have a far greater plan ahead of me, but right now it is impossible for me to see. No matter what the future brings, may I take heart that You are with me until the end of the age. Bring my family peace in the midst of this change, that we may not fear what is to come. Amen

Children are a gift from God, but that does not mean that their lives are entirely in their parents' hands. Remember that you are not perfect, and the safest place for your children is in the Father's hands. Lead them to the One who will never leave or betray them.

Sons are indeed a heritage from the LORD, *offspring, a reward. Like arrows in the hand of a warrior are the sons born in one's youth. Happy is the man who has filled his quiver with them. They will never be put to shame when they speak with their enemies at the city gate.*

    Psalm 127:3–5

———

Even a young man is known by his actions—by whether his behavior is pure and upright.

    Proverbs 20:11

When Jesus saw it, he was indignant and said to them, "Let the little children come to me. Don't stop them, because the kingdom of God belongs to such as these."

Mark 10:14

———

Fathers, don't stir up anger in your children, but bring them up in the training and instruction of the Lord.

Ephesians 6:4

———

Children, obey your parents in everything, for this pleases the Lord.

Colossians 3:20

Father, thank You for the blessing of my family. I praise You for my children. Lord, I want great things for them, and I know that I am incapable of raising them with You. Nothing I could do would ever be enough. I give them over to Your hands. Protect them, guide them, and give me the words to bring them up in Your instruction. Hold them to Your side that they may come to know You. Amen

None of us are immune from hardships, loss, and grief, but we can take heart that no matter what has happened, the Lord promises to comfort us. Sometimes He comforts us directly, sometimes through circumstances, and sometimes through the people He places in our families. Create your home as a place of comfort for your family.

Even when I go through the darkest valley, I fear no danger, for you are with me; your rod and your staff—they comfort me.

Psalm 23:4

———

Remember your word to your servant; you have given me hope through it. This is my comfort in my affliction: Your promise has given me life.

Psalm 119:49–50

———

As a mother comforts her son, so I will comfort you, and you will be comforted in Jerusalem.

Isaiah 66:13

"Blessed are those who mourn, for they will be comforted."

Matthew 5:4

———

Blessed be the God and Father of our Lord Jesus Christ, the Father of mercies and the God of all comfort. He comforts us in all our affliction, so that we may be able to comfort those who are in any kind of affliction, through the comfort we ourselves receive from God.

2 Corinthians 1:3–4

Dear God, thank You for comforting me and healing my heart in times of trial. Father, use me to bring comfort to my family. Help me to create a home that is inviting, welcoming, and reassuring to my family. That when they are home they feel peace from the chaos of the world. Give us the words to comfort each other, that our family can be life giving to one another. Amen

The Lord commands us to love our neighbors as ourselves and to also love our enemies— godly compassion is speaking and acting out of love in the best interests of others. Just like you would be willing to drop everything to help your dearest friend, you should be just as willing to have compassion for a stranger. This level of compassion is not possible on your own and is only possible through the Holy Spirit inside of you.

Yet he was compassionate; he atoned for their iniquity and did not destroy them. He often turned his anger aside and did not unleash all his wrath.

Psalm 78:38

———

When he went ashore, he saw a large crowd and had compassion on them, because they were like sheep without a shepherd. Then he began to teach them many things.

Mark 6:34

Carry one another's burdens; in this way you will fulfill the law of Christ.

Galatians 6:2

———

And be kind and compassionate to one another, forgiving one another, just as God also forgave you in Christ.

Ephesians 4:32

Lord, may Your Holy Spirit fill my heart and soul with concern for my family, friends, neighbors, colleagues, and even enemies. Father, sometimes it is difficult for me to have compassion on those I consider deserving of their grief. Remove this hate from within me. Help me to see people the way You see them and not through my own weaknesses. Open up my heart to the people around me that I may be a willing conduit of Your love. Amen

The longer you have been in any kind of relationship with someone, the more likely you have already experienced some kind of conflict with them. This is especially true for family members. Conflict can arise from any number of situations from pride, jealousy, misunderstanding, shame, or even just ignorance. One way we can walk in the Spirit, rather than according to the flesh, is to resist the pride and need to be right that we often feel in conflicts with others. Lay down your pride and allow your family to come together in peace.

Therefore, putting away lying, speak the truth, each one to his neighbor, because we are members of one another. Be angry and do not sin. Don't let the sun go down on your anger, and don't give the devil an opportunity.

    Ephesians 4:25–27

———

"If your brother sins against you, go and rebuke him in private. If he listens to you, you have won your brother. But if he won't listen, take one or two others with you, so that by the testimony of two or three witnesses every fact may be established. If he doesn't pay attention to them, tell the church. If he doesn't pay attention even to the church, let him be like a Gentile and a tax collector to you."

    Matthew 18:15–17

Bless those who persecute you; bless and do not curse. Rejoice with those who rejoice; weep with those who weep. Live in harmony with one another. Do not be proud; instead, associate with the humble. Do not be wise in your own estimation. Do not repay anyone evil for evil. Give careful thought to do what is honorable in everyone's eyes. If possible, as far as it depends on you, live at peace with everyone.

Romans 12:14–18

———

What is the source of wars and fights among you? Don't they come from your passions that wage war within you? You desire and do not have. You murder and covet and cannot obtain. You fight and wage war. You do not have because you do not ask.

James 4:1–2

Lord Jesus, my heart is full of conflict and resentment. Even after I claim to have forgiven my family members, I still hold on to the hurt and allow it to push me away from trust and into the throws of conflict. God, give me patience and peace. May I imitate Your grace and gentleness in every disagreement or confrontation with people in my life. Amen

While you may still be related, you lose relationship if you only talk to a family member once a year. It takes time, commitment, and devotion to the relationship. It is the same way with our relationships with God. We cannot show up at church on Sundays and expect that will be enough to have a relationship with our Father. If you truly care about someone, you desire to spend time with them, to learn them, to know their heart. As you read these verses, let them lead you into communion with the Father. Use them as a jumping off point for a life of devotion to Him.

This book of instruction must not depart from your mouth; you are to meditate on it day and night so that you may carefully observe everything written in it. For then you will prosper and succeed in whatever you do.

Joshua 1:8

———

"For where your treasure is, there your heart will be also."

Luke 12:34

"*No servant can serve two masters, since either he will hate one and love the other, or he will be devoted to one and despise the other. You cannot serve both God and money.*"
   Luke 16:13

———

Be diligent to present yourself to God as one approved, a worker who doesn't need to be ashamed, correctly teaching the word of truth.
   2 Timothy 2:15

Heavenly Father, I know that I do not spend as much time with You as I desire to. I allow my time to disappear as I spend it on the temporary while avoiding the eternal. Convict my heart and make me see my need for devoted time with You. Help me to set aside all distractions and listen to what You have to tell me. Amen

An essential path of growth is cultivating self-discipline: do the right thing at the right time in the right way. It is also the biggest way to alleviate stress. When you have a disciplined life, you do not need to worry about what will happen because you are already prepared in the places you have control and can leave the rest up to God. Of course, discipline is painful at the time; but if it is for training in the Lord's way, it will result in righteousness.

Whoever loves discipline loves knowledge, but one who hates correction is stupid.

Proverbs 12:1

———

The one who will not use the rod hates his son, but the one who loves him disciplines him diligently.

Proverbs 13:24

———

Foolishness is bound to the heart of a youth; a rod of discipline will separate it from him.

Proverbs 22:15

Instead, I discipline my body and bring it under strict control, so that after preaching to others, I myself will not be disqualified.

1 Corinthians 9:27

———

No discipline seems enjoyable at the time, but painful. Later on, however, it yields the peaceful fruit of righteousness to those who have been trained by it.

Hebrews 12:11

Heavenly Father, may Your hand guide me and correct me so that all I do and say will glorify You. Help me to live a life that is disciplined and steady. Give me the skills I need so that I can stay true to Your training. Give me guidance in the way I discipline my children. Help me to never act out of anger, but only out of love. Amen

God places people in our lives for a reason and for our good. Seek out those who bring you encouragement. Pray for those you can bring encouragement to. Never hold in kindness that can be spread to lift up those around you. You never know when those words are God pouring out encouragement through you to others.

The L<small>ORD</small> is the one who will go before you. He will be with you; he will not leave you or abandon you. Do not be afraid or discouraged.

    Deuteronomy 31:8

———

God is our refuge and strength, a helper who is always found in times of trouble.

    Psalm 46:1

———

"Aren't five sparrows sold for two pennies? Yet not one of them is forgotten in God's sight. Indeed, the hairs of your head are all counted. Don't be afraid; you are worth more than many sparrows."

    Luke 12:6–7

"*I have told you these things so that in me you may have peace. You will have suffering in this world. Be courageous! I have conquered the world.*"
    John 16:33

———

And let us watch out for one another to provoke love and good works, not neglecting to gather together, as some are in the habit of doing, but encouraging each other, and all the more as you see the day approaching.
    Hebrews 10:24–25

Christ Jesus, may Your Spirit strengthen and encourage my heart today. Comfort me in my grief, and show me those around me who need my encouragement. Place on my heart those friends and relatives who need a kind word today. Allow me to be the tool You use to help lift up everyone I meet today. Amen

Families come in all shapes and sizes. They bring out our best and our worst. They are filled with bonds that can never be broken and heartache from deeply rooted hurts. The family was created by God, and He has given us some guidelines to help us flourish, to honor one another, and to push each other into Christ's arms.

Honor your father and your mother so that you may have a long life in the land that the LORD your God is giving you.

Exodus 20:12

———

Sons are indeed a heritage from the LORD, offspring, a reward. Like arrows in the hand of a warrior are the sons born in one's youth. Happy is the man who has filled his quiver with them. They will never be put to shame when they speak with their enemies at the city gate.

Psalm 127:3–5

Wives, submit to your husbands as to the Lord, because the husband is the head of the wife as Christ is the head of the church. He is the Savior of the body. Now as the church submits to Christ, so also wives are to submit to their husbands in everything. Husbands, love your wives, just as Christ loved the church and gave himself for her to make her holy, cleansing her with the washing of water by the word. He did this to present the church to himself in splendor, without spot or wrinkle or anything like that, but holy and blameless. In the same way, husbands are to love their wives as their own bodies. He who loves his wife loves himself.

    Ephesians 5:22–28

———

Fathers, don't stir up anger in your children, but bring them up in the training and instruction of the Lord.

    Ephesians 6:4

Father, thank You for the blessing You have given me of my family. I know I sometimes take them for granted and do not treat them as well as I should. I ask forgiveness for these transgressions against them. Please help keep me accountable for my actions towards my family. Help me to see and meet their needs. Bless them and keep them safe. Amen

Fear comes in many forms; fear of the unknown, of the impossible, of broken trust. Any of these fears can be all consuming. But we have an almighty God who loves us and cares for us at all times. We have a powerful God who is strong through all things. We have an omnipresent God who never leaves us alone, and a God who is greater than any of our fears. With God on our side, there is nothing to fear, and nothing to stand in our way.

Haven't I commanded you: be strong and courageous? Do not be afraid or discouraged, for the LORD your God is with you wherever you go.

Joshua 1:9

———

When I am afraid, I will trust in you.

Psalm 56:3

———

You did not receive a spirit of slavery to fall back into fear. Instead, you received the Spirit of adoption, by whom we cry out, "Abba, Father!"

Romans 8:15

For God has not given us a spirit of fear, but one of power, love, and sound judgment.

    2 Timothy 1:7

————

Humble yourselves, therefore, under the mighty hand of God, so that he may exalt you at the proper time, casting all your cares on him, because he cares about you.

    1 Peter 5:6–7

Abba, Father, I cry out to You for Your protection and comfort. I'm overwhelmed with fear—fear of the future and the unknown. I know that my fear stems from distrust, and that if I truly trusted You the way I say I do, then I would not have any fear. Thank You for Your faithful love and comfort. Continue to shelter me when I feel afraid. Amen

Constantly busy with work, children, school, and other obligations, finding family time can be difficult. When you do not intentionally schedule it into your week, it can become a thing of the past. But it is important to refresh your heart and soul. Find time this week to be with your family, not as an obligation or with any agenda, but just to fill your cup.

Iron sharpens iron, and one person sharpens another.

> *Proverbs 27:17*

———

Two are better than one because they have a good reward for their efforts. For if either falls, his companion can lift him up; but pity the one who falls without another to lift him up.

> *Ecclesiastes 4:9–10*

———

Carry one another's burdens; in this way you will fulfill the law of Christ.

> *Galatians 6:2*

Therefore encourage one another and build each other up as you are already doing.
    1 Thessalonians 5:11

———

And let us watch out for one another to provoke love and good works, not neglecting to gather together, as some are in the habit of doing, but encouraging each other, and all the more as you see the day approaching.
    Hebrews 10:24–25

Dear Jesus, please reveal to me ways I can spend more time in fellowship with my family, building each other up. Show me the times in my schedule where I need to create margin to spend with the people who refresh my soul. Allow my presence to be a blessing to others. Amen

Forgiving someone who has hurt you means you no longer call to mind their fault or error—this extends grace to them and freedom for you. But it is not something that comes naturally, or easily, especially when the hurt has been caused by someone you trusted. This level of forgiveness is only possible by leaning on the Holy Spirit within you, and allowing Him to take control of cleaning your heart.

"Therefore I tell you, her many sins have been forgiven; that's why she loved much. But the one who is forgiven little, loves little."

   Luke 7:47

———

Live in harmony with one another. Do not be proud; instead, associate with the humble. Do not be wise in your own estimation. Do not repay anyone evil for evil. Give careful thought to do what is honorable in everyone's eyes. If possible, as far as it depends on you, live at peace with everyone.

   Romans 12:16–18

Be kind and compassionate to one another,
forgiving one another, just as God also forgave you
in Christ.
    Ephesians 4:32

———

As God's chosen ones, holy and dearly loved, put on
compassion, kindness, humility, gentleness, and
patience, bearing with one another and forgiving
one another if anyone has a grievance against
another. Just as the Lord has forgiven you, so you
are also to forgive.
    Colossians 3:12–13

Dear God, it is easy for me to say that I forgive my family, but to actually release the resentment from my heart and let it be as if nothing ever happened . . . well I do not have any idea how to do that. Sometimes I feel trapped by the grudges and feelings of hurt that I have chosen to hold on to. I know that the feelings are not only damaging me, but my relationships as well. Please, just as You forgave all my debts and wrongs through Christ, empower me to extend forgiveness to those who have mistreated or hurt me. Amen

What does happiness look like to you?
Is it a good book on the back porch? Or a hike
in the mountains with your family? Maybe
it's sitting around a campfire laughing with
old friends. Though happiness sometimes
comes from external circumstances, we
experience the most lasting happiness by
enjoying our union with Christ.

Therefore my heart is glad and my whole being rejoices; my body also rests securely.

   Psalm 16:9

———

Take delight in the LORD, and he will give you your heart's desires.

   Psalm 37:4

A joyful heart makes a face cheerful, but a sad heart produces a broken spirit.

> *Proverbs 15:13*

———

I know that there is nothing better for them than to rejoice and enjoy the good life.

> *Ecclesiastes 3:12*

———

Rejoice in the Lord always. I will say it again: Rejoice!

> *Philippians 4:4*

Lord Jesus, I know that Your desire is for me to be happy. Align the desires of my heart with Your desires, so that I may find full and complete happiness. May my heart be happy and cheerful because I know You. Amen

One of the foundations of a strong friendship is honesty. You cannot have a fruitful relationship without it. Your friends need to know that they can rely on your word and know that you speak truth. It can feel easier to lie, to protect yourself from others by covering yourself with deceit, but this will only lead to heartbreak and destruction. Complete honesty is not possible without the Holy Spirit leading your words and actions. Give Him full control today.

Who is someone who desires life, loving a long life
to enjoy what is good? Keep your tongue from evil
and your lips from deceitful speech. Turn away from
evil and do what is good; seek peace and pursue it.

    Psalm 34:12–14

———

Better a poor person who lives with integrity than
someone who has deceitful lips and is a fool.

    Proverbs 19:1

———

"But let your 'yes' mean 'yes,' and your 'no' mean
'no.' Anything more than this is from the evil one."

    Matthew 5:37

Indeed, we are giving careful thought to do what is right, not only before the Lord but also before people.

   2 Corinthians 8:21

———

Do not lie to one another, since you have put off the old self with its practices.

   Colossians 3:9

Father, lies flow from my lips as easily as air. I change stories, hide feelings, and even gossip about things I know nothing about. I know it is only with Your help that I can remove this sin from my life. Father, guard my tongue that I may no longer speak anything but the truth. Convict me of the deception that I have released, and forgive me for the untrue things I have said. Amen

There is a balance that many people find themselves in, trying to counter-balance their pride by putting themselves down. This is not the same as humility. The key to cultivating true humility isn't to act self-deprecating but to simply not think of oneself much at all; to recognize that it is not about us, but only about God; and to give importance to others simply because they are God's creation and deserve to be treated as such.

Sitting down, he called the Twelve and said to them, "If anyone wants to be first, he must be last and servant of all."

Mark 9:35

———

Live in harmony with one another. Do not be proud; instead, associate with the humble. Do not be wise in your own estimation.

Romans 12:16

———

Do nothing out of selfish ambition or conceit, but in humility consider others as more important than yourselves.

Philippians 2:3

Adopt the same attitude as that of Christ Jesus, who, existing in the form of God, did not consider equality with God as something to be exploited. Instead he emptied himself by assuming the form of a servant, taking on the likeness of humanity. And when he had come as a man, he humbled himself by becoming obedient to the point of death—even to death on a cross.

    Philippians 2:5–8

———

Who among you is wise and understanding? By his good conduct he should show that his works are done in the gentleness that comes from wisdom.

    James 3:13

Lord Jesus, who demonstrated perfect selflessness, please be my vision and my constant focus so that I forget myself completely. It is so easy for me to shift my focus onto myself, and even when I try to correct, I do so by putting myself down. Let me be so consumed by You that there are no thoughts left for myself. Amen

Impulsive behavior is what flows out of your heart without thought or reflection. The feeling that most reliably follows an impulsive word or action is regret, because our hearts are full of sinful desires. Choose instead to be patient and deliberate. Fill yourself with wisdom, so that when an impulsive decision is needed, what flows out instinctively is God's Word and not your own.

Discretion will watch over you, and understanding will guard you. It will rescue you from the way of evil—from anyone who says perverse things,
   Proverbs 2:11–12

———

So if you have been raised with Christ, seek the things above, where Christ is, seated at the right hand of God. Set your minds on things above, not on earthly things.
   Colossians 3:1–2

For we all stumble in many ways. If anyone does not stumble in what he says, he is mature, able also to control the whole body.

    James 3:2

———

Watch yourselves so you don't lose what we have worked for, but that you may receive a full reward. Anyone who does not remain in Christ's teaching but goes beyond it does not have God. The one who remains in that teaching, this one has both the Father and the Son.

    2 John 8–9

Lord God, when I am living in the urgent, my heart turns back to my sinful ways. I do the things I don't want to do, and I don't do the things I want to do. Father, I need Your help to cut away my impulsive behavior. Fill me with Your wisdom, so that I am protected from my own sinful desires. Control my words and actions, that I may not sin against You. Amen

In God's great kindness, He saved us through His beloved Son, and He now calls us to extend that same gentleness and compassion to others, regardless of what excuses we come up with from our own lives. Look for opportunities, even in the midst of high levels of stress, to bestow kindness to the members of your family. Look for ways to bless them in simple ways that show them how much you care.

*He also raised us up with him and seated us with
him in the heavens in Christ Jesus, so that in the
coming ages he might display the immeasurable
riches of his grace through his kindness to us in
Christ Jesus.*

   Ephesians 2:6–7

———

*Let all bitterness, anger and wrath, shouting and
slander be removed from you, along with all malice.
And be kind and compassionate to one another,
forgiving one another, just as God also forgave you
in Christ.*

   Ephesians 4:31–32

Therefore, as God's chosen ones, holy and dearly loved, put on compassion, kindness, humility, gentleness, and patience.

Colossians 3:12

———

But when the kindness of God our Savior and his love for mankind appeared, he saved us—not by works of righteousness that we had done, but according to his mercy—through the washing of regeneration and renewal by the Holy Spirit.

Titus 3:4–6

Dear God, may Your Holy Spirit soften my speech and actions so that I display Your kindness towards everyone. I know I have failed and allowed my circumstances to take control of my reactions, but I want to repent and give my reactions over to Your control. Open my eyes to the opportunities around me to show kindness to my family. Amen

Even surrounded by people it is easy to feel alone. Thanks to social media, the fast-paced modern life has left many of us feeling isolated—but thanks to God's faithful presence and our community of believers, we never have to be alone. Jesus will never leave you or cancel plans. He is always available for you when you need Him.

"My presence will go with you, and I will give you rest."

    Exodus 33:14

———

The LORD is the one who will go before you. He will be with you; he will not leave you or abandon you. Do not be afraid or discouraged.

    Deuteronomy 31:8

———

God provides homes for those who are deserted. He leads out the prisoners to prosperity, but the rebellious live in a scorched land.

    Psalm 68:6

*He heals the brokenhearted and bandages their
wounds.*

   Psalm 147:3

———

*Blessed be the God and Father of our Lord Jesus
Christ, the Father of mercies and the God of all
comfort. He comforts us in all our affliction, so that
we may be able to comfort those who are in any
kind of affliction, through the comfort we ourselves
receive from God.*

   2 Corinthians 1:3–4

Father of mercies, please comfort me in times of loneliness so that I may be a comfort to others. Remind me that even in my deepest despair, no matter where I am, You are with me. Thank You for being a constant reminder that I am never alone. Continue to hold me in Your arms, and help me to be a shoulder for others to help them know that I am here for them. Amen

Our highest calling is to love God with all of our heart, our soul, and our mind, and to love our neighbor as ourselves. But what does it mean to love your neighbor as yourself? It is easy to love our friends, but enemies are a whole other story. Only with God's love in our hearts are we able to truly love all people.

But I say to you who listen: Love your enemies, do what is good to those who hate you, bless those who curse you, pray for those who mistreat you.

    Luke 6:27–28

———

Love is patient, love is kind. Love does not envy, is not boastful, is not arrogant, is not rude, is not self-seeking, is not irritable, and does not keep a record of wrongs.

    1 Corinthians 13:4–5

———

Above all, maintain constant love for one another, since love covers a multitude of sins.

    1 Peter 4:8

God's love was revealed among us in this way: God sent his one and only Son into the world so that we might live through him.

    1 John 4:9

————

And we have come to know and to believe the love that God has for us. God is love, and the one who remains in love remains in God, and God remains in him.

    1 John 4:16

Dear Jesus, there are people in my life that it is hard for me to love. I know that I am still called to love them, but it seems impossible without Your guidance. Instill in my heart the selfless concern and compassion for others that You demonstrated for me. Help me to love people with Your love, and not with what I am capable of on my own. Amen

The covenantal union between a man and a woman is a symbol of our ultimate hope—the consummation of our union with the Lord Jesus. But that does not mean it is always easy. Marriage was not given to us to make us complete, or make us happy. No one is saved by marriage; they are saved by Jesus Christ alone. Marriage is a means by which God sanctifies people who He has called to the union.

*This is why a man leaves his father and mother and
bonds with his wife, and they become one flesh.*

Genesis 2:24

———

*A man who finds a wife finds a good thing
and obtains favor from the* LORD.

Proverbs 18:22

———

*Marriage is to be honored by all and the marriage
bed kept undefiled, because God will judge the
sexually immoral and adulterers.*

Hebrews 13:4

Wives, submit to your husbands as to the Lord, because the husband is the head of the wife as Christ is the head of the church. He is the Savior of the body. Now as the church submits to Christ, so also wives are to submit to their husbands in everything. Husbands, love your wives, just as Christ loved the church and gave himself for her to make her holy, cleansing her with the washing of water by the word. . . . In the same way, husbands are to love their wives as their own bodies. He who loves his wife loves himself. For no one ever hates his own flesh but provides and cares for it, just as Christ does for the church, since we are members of his body. For this reason a man will leave his father and mother and be joined to his wife, and the two will become one flesh. This mystery is profound, but I am talking about Christ and the church. To sum up, each one of you is to love his wife as himself, and the wife is to respect her husband.

    Ephesians 5:22–33

Heavenly Father, thank You for the gift of a spouse, and the blessings You have brought into our relationship. God, You know that we are both sinful people, and we would not be able to love one another and serve in this relationship if it was not for the guidance and grace that You have poured out on us. Continue to guide our steps in this family, and hold us to our vows. May we love and support one another just as You love and strengthen Your church. Amen

Money is an essential and valuable tool, but too much trust in it or desire for it can quickly lead us away from what's most important. Are you causing grief in your family because of the importance that you place on money? Or is it something else that you are rapidly chasing after? Relinquish your search for what the world considers success, and pursue the higher calling of Jesus Christ. Push yourself toward God's will alone.

"No one can serve two masters, since either he will hate one and love the other, or he will be devoted to one and despise the other. You cannot serve both God and money."

Matthew 6:24

———

Pay your obligations to everyone: taxes to those you owe taxes, tolls to those you owe tolls, respect to those you owe respect, and honor to those you owe honor.

Romans 13:7

For the love of money is a root of all kinds of evil, and by craving it, some have wandered away from the faith and pierced themselves with many griefs.

1 Timothy 6:10

———

Instruct those who are rich in the present age not to be arrogant or to set their hope on the uncertainty of wealth, but on God, who richly provides us with all things to enjoy.

1 Timothy 6:17

———

Keep your life free from the love of money. Be satisfied with what you have, for he himself has said, "I will never leave you or abandon you."

Hebrews 13:5

Heavenly Father, who richly provides us with so much abundance, please keep my heart free from covetousness and the love of money. I want to believe that my desires are only for Your will, but again and again I find myself back at the alter of finance. Lord, continue to remind me of my need for redemption. Help me to let go of the idol of financial stability that I have created, and replace it with faith that You will provide for all of my needs. Amen

While other people can only see our actions, God can look at our hearts and see the motives behind what we do. Rather than self-seeking or people pleasing, we should endeavor to do all things through genuine love for God and others. But that can be harder than it sounds. Use these verses to remind yourself of the importance of what is in your heart.

But the LORD said to Samuel, "Do not look at his appearance or his stature because I have rejected him. Humans do not see what the LORD sees, for humans see what is visible, but the LORD sees the heart."

1 Samuel 16:7

———

All a person's ways seem right to him, but the LORD weighs hearts.

Proverbs 21:2

———

For am I now trying to persuade people, or God? Or am I striving to please people? If I were still trying to please people, I would not be a servant of Christ.

Galatians 1:10

Do nothing out of selfish ambition or conceit, but in humility consider others as more important than yourselves.

    Philippians 2:3

———

Instead, just as we have been approved by God to be entrusted with the gospel, so we speak, not to please people, but rather God, who examines our hearts.

    1 Thessalonians 2:4

Lord, please weigh my heart and my reasons for doing the things I do, and reveal to me any motives that don't glorify You. Help me to pull out those motives and change them. Give me a genuine love for the people around me, and move my heart to be so focused on You that everything I do is glorifying to Your name. Amen

The liveliness of children or the demands of the workplace can rattle your nerves, but take care to avoid making wrong choices or damaging your relationships. Remember the amount of patience that God has given you in your life, and pass it on to the people around you. Not one of us is perfect, and we all need grace and time to find the right path.

The end of a matter is better than its beginning; a patient spirit is better than a proud spirit.

Ecclesiastes 7:8

———

Now if we hope for what we do not see, we eagerly wait for it with patience.

Romans 8:25

———

My dear brothers and sisters, understand this: Everyone should be quick to listen, slow to speak, and slow to anger, for human anger does not accomplish God's righteousness.

James 1:19–20

Therefore, brothers and sisters, be patient until the Lord's coming. See how the farmer waits for the precious fruit of the earth and is patient with it until it receives the early and the late rains. You also must be patient. Strengthen your hearts, because the Lord's coming is near.

James 5:7–8

———

The Lord does not delay his promise, as some understand delay, but is patient with you, not wanting any to perish but all to come to repentance.

2 Peter 3:9

Heavenly Father, You are patient and slow to anger—please help me be still and wait patiently for You. When I start to lose my way and my temper, give me Your calming touch, and help me to take a step back and remember what is really important. Thank You for the strength that You lend to me when I do not have enough by myself. Amen

Pride comes in many shapes and sizes.
Arrogance tells us we are better than others,
low self-esteem tells us we are worse, and
praise makes us feel important, but they are all
signs of pride, because they all put the focus
on ourselves. Though we may be blessed with
wisdom, success, and happy relationships, we
can avoid pride by remembering that all good
things are ours by the grace of God.

When arrogance comes, disgrace follows, but with humility comes wisdom.
Proverbs 11:2

———

Everyone with a proud heart is detestable to the LORD; be assured, he will not go unpunished.
Proverbs 16:5

———

A person's pride will humble him, but a humble spirit will gain honor.
Proverbs 29:23

Live in harmony with one another. Do not be proud; instead, associate with the humble. Do not be wise in your own estimation.

Romans 12:16

———

For if anyone considers himself to be something when he is nothing, he deceives himself.

Galatians 6:3

Father God, please forgive the ways I puff myself up rather than humble myself under Your loving hand. Help me to forget about myself, and keep my eyes on You. When I fall into a trap of pride, pull me to repentance, that I may not continue to sin against You. I know that any good I am capable of is only because of You. Amen

Loving relationships and friendships are gifts from God—we are built up and supported in community and in fellowship with other believers. We must be intentional within those relationships, or they will fall under the weight of sin. Look for ways today to strengthen the relationships that you have, and opportunities to grow new ones.

Iron sharpens iron, and one person sharpens another.

   Proverbs 27:17

―――――

Two are better than one because they have a good reward for their efforts. For if either falls, his companion can lift him up; but pity the one who falls without another to lift him up.

   Ecclesiastes 4:9–10

―――――

Carry one another's burdens; in this way you will fulfill the law of Christ.

   Galatians 6:2

Don't become partners with those who do not believe. For what partnership is there between righteousness and lawlessness? Or what fellowship does light have with darkness?

  2 Corinthians 6:14

———

Therefore encourage one another and build each other up as you are already doing.

  1 Thessalonians 5:11

———

Above all, maintain constant love for one another, since love covers a multitude of sins.

  1 Peter 4:8

Heavenly Father, reveal to me ways I can be a conduit of Your love toward those in my community today. Open my eyes to relationships that need my attention, and opportunities to love others the way that You have called me to love them. If I have any broken relationships, pull me to repentance, that I may show Your glory in redemption. Amen

Any relationship can cause stress, but families in particular are a breading ground for anxiety. Chronic stress is quickly becoming a national crisis that threatens our health—but God is our ever-present helper in times of trouble. Lay your burdens at His feet, and do not allow yourself to become overwhelmed with the temporary problems of this world. Cast your burdens on Him, and He will carry you through this time of stress.

Cast your burden on the LORD, and he will sustain you; he will never allow the righteous to be shaken.

Psalm 55:22

———

Commit your activities to the LORD, and your plans will be established.

Proverbs 16:3

———

For I am the LORD your God, who holds your right hand, who says to you, "Do not fear, I will help you."

Isaiah 41:13

Come to me, all of you who are weary and burdened, and I will give you rest. Take up my yoke and learn from me, because I am lowly and humble in heart, and you will find rest for your souls. For my yoke is easy and my burden is light.

Matthew 11:28–30

———

I am able to do all things through him who strengthens me.

Philippians 4:13

Dear God, please fill me and strengthen me with Your Spirit when I feel overwhelmed, exhausted, and uncertain. My family causes me constant stress. I know that it is because of the amount of love I have for them, but sometimes I become overwhelmed. Give me peace during the stress. Remind me daily of what You have trusted me to handle, and what I need to lay down at Your feet. Help me to trust You and to know that nothing I do can ever get in the way of Your plan. Amen

Trust is not an easy thing to give away.
Everyone has had a time when their trust has
been given to a friend, only to be betrayed. But
God is not a fallible human. To trust the Lord
is to believe what He has said about Himself—
He is good, faithful, and sovereign. He is
always worthy and deserving of our trust.

The person who trusts in the LORD, *whose confidence indeed is the* LORD, *is blessed. He will be like a tree planted by water: it sends its roots out toward a stream, it doesn't fear when heat comes, and its foliage remains green. It will not worry in a year of drought or cease producing fruit.*

Jeremiah 17:7–8

———

Wait for the LORD; *be strong, and let your heart be courageous. Wait for the* LORD.

Psalm 27:14

———

And my God will supply all your needs according to his riches in glory in Christ Jesus.

Philippians 4:19

I will be with you when you pass through the waters, and when you pass through the rivers, they will not overwhelm you. You will not be scorched when you walk through the fire, and the flame will not burn you.

Isaiah 43:2

———

This is the confidence we have before him: If we ask anything according to his will, he hears us.

1 John 5:14

Dear God, thank You that all things work together for the good of those who love You and are called according to Your purpose. Amen

Though we may have advanced degrees and years of experience, this without the Spirit gives us only knowledge and not true wisdom with what to do with the information. The Holy Spirit, who helps us discern what is true, good, and right, will bless you with wisdom when you seek Him. Study the Scriptures, so that when you are in times of trial, wisdom pours out of your heart.

Teach us to number our days carefully so that we may develop wisdom in our hearts.

    Psalm 90:12

———

Do not be conformed to this age, but be transformed by the renewing of your mind, so that you may discern what is the good, pleasing, and perfect will of God.

    Romans 12:2

Yet to those who are called, both Jews and Greeks, Christ is the power of God and the wisdom of God, because God's foolishness is wiser than human wisdom, and God's weakness is stronger than human strength.

    1 Corinthians 1:24–25

———

Now if any of you lacks wisdom, he should ask God—who gives to all generously and ungrudgingly—and it will be given to him.

    James 1:5

Heavenly Father, who gives generously and freely, please fill me with Your wisdom for how to be righteous. Guide my steps, and transform my mind, that I may see the world with Your eyes and truly understand what is at stake behind sinful decisions. Father, teach me to be wise, that I may not stray from Your side. Amen

Worry is false and useless fear—it's imagining and anticipating what might happen but probably won't. What can you change by worrying about it? Nothing. What can you fix by thinking about everything that could go wrong? Nothing. Instead, spend your time focused on today. On what you can do, on what you know to be truth, and leave the rest to God.

*"Therefore I tell you: Don't worry about your life,
what you will eat or what you will drink; or about
your body, what you will wear. Isn't life more than
food and the body more than clothing? Consider the
birds of the sky: They don't sow or reap or gather
into barns, yet your heavenly Father feeds them.
Aren't you worth more than they? Can any of you
add one moment to his life-span by worrying?"*

    Matthew 6:25–27

———

*The Lord answered her, "Martha, Martha, you are
worried and upset about many things, but one
thing is necessary. Mary has made the right choice,
and it will not be taken away from her."*

    Luke 10:41–42

We know that all things work together for the good of those who love God, who are called according to his purpose.

    Romans 8:28

———

Don't worry about anything, but in everything, through prayer and petition with thanksgiving, present your requests to God. And the peace of God, which surpasses all understanding, will guard your hearts and minds in Christ Jesus.

    Philippians 4:6–7

Lord Jesus, I am often worried about many things. I worry about tomorrow, about my family, about what friends are really thinking, about health, about clothes, about money, and about countless other meaningless things. Jesus, I know that my worry with do nothing, but the thoughts are rooted in my mind, and I know I cannot remove them without Your help. Remind me of Your provision. Show me ways to let go of my worry. Please grant me a heart like Mary, who rested at Your feet. Amen